LAMENTING SAM

By Kelly Jo Terry

Book Cover Formatting: Tara Richter

Interior Book Formatting: Kaitlyn Sanderson

Book Cover Artwork: Justin Miller

Editors: Haley Cox

Proof Reader: Steven Tye

Publisher: Richter Publishing LLC www.richterpublishing.com

ISBN-13:978-1-954094-76-5

DISCLAIMER

DEDICATION

I dedicate this book to my love, my partner in crime, my rock and the one who walked by my side day after day to keep me alive. John, your constant love, support and strength provided me the space and freedom to journey through the early years of grief with protection and grace. I am forever grateful for your endless patience and love. I love you 4-ever!

TABLE OF CONTENTS

ACKNOWLEDGMENTS

Thank you, Tara and Haley, at Richter Publishing for your guidance and expertise and for believing in the healing power of poetry in grief. Thank you, too, for your endless patience with a writer who is hopelessly trapped in the age of analogue.

A special and most heartfelt thank you to my tribe.

My Starfish

The Friday Church Ladies

The Earliest Years Divas

My chosen sisters

The SSIX

The BFFL family

The Arrawana Krewe

My beloved Jaates

My Mother-in-Law

My Family

I thank you all for feeding me and mine, body and soul, in those dreadful first months. Thank you for every tear-filled day and wine-filled night. For Holy Spirit moments on the kitchen floor and for your endless prayers, understanding and patience.

And finally, thank you to all who continue to support and love me on this dreadful, beautiful, painful and magical journey to becoming "me."

PREFACE

"In the English language there are orphans and widows, but there is no word for the parents who lose a child." —Jodi Picoult, "My Sister's Keeper"

On February 7, 2020, I found my beloved son, Sam, on his bedroom floor. He was gone. And in that instant, so was the world as I knew it. Overcome with grief and all the trappings that come along with it, I became unrecognizable to myself and moved through the days as though I was entangled in a dank and weighty shroud. I could not eat nor sleep and truly believed that I would never know real joy again. As a visual artist and painter, my will to create was gone with my boy, and with no outlet to express my suffering, I was adrift.

Then, one day, someone gifted me a series of small books on grief that included a few pages for journaling one's feelings. Near hopeless and knowing that I had to find a way to release the myriad of feelings swirling inside my mind, I began to pour them out onto the page. Those first words became pages, then journals, then volumes, and I began to see a flicker of light in the darkness that had enveloped me. The pen had replaced the paintbrush and lined paper became my new canvas.

What flowed out of my very cells and marrow were poems and pieces of prose that helped me learn to honor my pain, to embrace my new reality and to be able to feel joy again as a stronger, better version of myself. One that, I know, Sammy is proud of.

My sincerest hope is that my words and musings can reach into the darkness of someone's suffering and give them the courage to keep going and reach for the light.

My heart is a relentless pounding muscle filled with millions of broken pieces. Sleep and I are strangers, for now. I breathe and move and speak and sob and laugh because my father in heaven is holding me up and my precious husband and all my beautiful friends and family are present and helpful and prayerful and attempting to feed me. And because my Emily, Austin, Jesse, Aubrey and TJ are suffering too and they need their mama.

I am existing because I know that my Bubby is with his beloved Abuela and, as TJ said, "probably having one of the best movie nights ever." I know he is always with me and I will be with him, a long time from now, again one day. And I am so grateful that he is continuously making his presence known.

Ours is a magical love story. He was a brightly burning star that was too loving, too sensitive, too gifted, too brilliant, too passionate, too curious and too loyal for this planet we call home. Somewhere inside I've always known our time together was limited. He was just always too big. And that smile... please remember that smile. And how fiercely he loved us. How he could (as his great grandmother Davis once noted) "talk the horns off a Billy goat," make you laugh, piss you off, try to convince you that your "blue" wasn't his "blue" so that the sky wasn't actually blue, and talk endlessly about his ridiculously vivid dreams. Remember that he was a brilliant artist, talented musician, writer and poet. How he is the best son, bonus son, grandson, brother, cousin, nephew, friend and cat dad that this world will ever know. And that he made me a better mama and human.

I love you forever, my beautiful boy! Until we meet again... have fun, be safe, and make good choices.

KJT 02.09.2020

"...bone of my bones and flesh of my flesh, she shall be called woman..." —Genesis 2:23

"It will be like a woman suffering the pains of labor. When her child is born, her anguish gives way to joy because she has brought a new baby into the world." —John 16:21

These verses have been on my mind. Contemplatively. Angrily. Sadly. It's as though our Heavenly Father missed a part. Especially for the mamas.

I know He didn't. I know He couldn't. Wouldn't.

But when we grow our babies, right in the tender part in our bellies, under our hearts, they are not only "bone of our bones" and "flesh of our flesh." They are the "heart of our heart" down to the very "cell of our cells." We are, forever, that entwined. And when one of our babies goes Home, unnaturally, before we do we are doubly cursed. Cursed with pain of childbirth then cursed again with the agony of our very cells simultaneously collapsing and exploding under the unbearable weight of loss. But this time there is no forgetting. No joy. No safety net. It's so easy to think He missed something. He forgot us. Faith, for now, just isn't enough. It simply won't do.

But then the angels appear. The goddesses. The sister-mamas. The ones who can only imagine the pain. The women who can't bear to imagine the pain but who dive headfirst into it for their devastated sister. The soul sisters who wade through the anguish when every cell in their body implores them to run as fast as they can in the opposite direction because it's all too horrible. Too painful. Too close. Too possible. But they don't. They show up. They stay. They weep. They feed. They clean. They come back, again and again. They stay. They hold. They lift up. They let in. They laugh. And they bring wine and love. So, so much love.

These are my cell-sisters. My angels. My soul's sisters. My sisters in Christ. They are the reason I and my precious, strong, loving, supportive rock of a husband and our beautiful children are still standing. Still breathing. They are Heaven sent. THEY are the safety net He planned for and I am beyond and forever grateful.

I love you, all you beautiful goddesses. Thank you for loving me and mine as if we are the "bone of your bones and the flesh of your flesh."

KJT 02.13.2020

"Then he took Jesus' body down, wrapped it in linen cloth and laid it in a tomb, one in which no one had yet been laid. It was Preparation Day and the Sabbath was about to begin. The women who had come with Jesus from Galilee followed Joseph and saw the tomb and how his body was laid in it. Then they went home and prepared spices and perfumes..."
—Luke 23:53-56

I've been drawn to these verses. Remembering how, as a child in Baptist school, I thought it so strange, so creepy, so weird for Mary and Mary and Mary and Joana to prepare "spices and perfumes" to anoint our precious Christ.

Fast forward 40 or so years, as I mourn the loss of my boy, and all of the love and desire and passion flood over me to honor his precious body just as women have done through the ages. A desire so deep that it stirred my first taste of rage, my first experience with the "anger" stage of grief. But I wasn't angry at Sammy or at God or the universe. I was angry at what dying and death has become. Something to fear. Something to avoid. Something to look away from and hand over to the "professionals".

So I read these words and I prayed over them. And I researched how we, as humans, have loved and honored and adored our dead through the ages. And, I did what I could. I demanded to see my baby, to kiss his sweet face and tell him how much I love him. How I've always loved him and always will. And how sorry I was, for those of us left here without him, that it turned out this way. Then, before I let him go, I begged for a lock of his beloved curly hair.

Oooooh, that hair. He loved and babied that gorgeous hair. Deep-golden ringlets that smelled of his Auntie Deedee's "mermaid oil."

Then I prayed and raged and wailed and prayed again and again. Knowing (most of the time) that God was listening and that He would give 7 times 7 times.

Last Friday, they called to tell us that Sammy's ashes and his lock of hair were ready to be picked up. And so we went. God only knows HOW we went. And when we got back in the car, in what can only be called a fugue state, I counted the locks. Seven! & big, thick, curly locks all in their own little packages.

So I looked at my boy's locks. And I looked and touched and I thanked God for the gift of them. And then I knew. Deep down in the broken and raging and prayerful and honoring place in my soul, I knew.

I prepared a bowl of warm water filled with his favorite shampoo and I washed his hair. I slowly and gratefully washed each wonderful strand. I ran a warm water stream and rinsed then conditioned it (leaving it in for 2-3 minutes, just like he said he did) and rinsed again. And then, just as so many women have done in generations before... I prepared the spices and perfumes from Auntie Deedee and I anointed our boy.

We are made in His image and we are completely and endlessly loved.

KJT 02.20.2020

Always praying for a good word to come to me... to move through me. I've spoken, of late, of my "lack of vision" or "lack of hopes for the future" with regards to my Bubby. An unconscious knowing, perhaps, that our time together, our love story, was to be short lived. Not in any prophetic or dramatic sense. Nothing ever focused on or obsessed over. Nothing ever even realized until, well, it was realized. I think this might cause some confusion and undue pain so I've been praying about it for weeks. And tonight, the proverbial "lightbulb" came on.

You know how when one of those pretty, decorative bulbs go out on a chandelier? You can't ignore it. It demands your attention. Then, when you get up on the ladder and go to change it, it lights up, brighter than before, the instant you touch it. You know that it's probably burning out. So brightly and so beautifully. But you leave it. Gently tightening it into its safe place. And you slowly back away, hoping it will survive, shining brightly for a while longer...

That was me and my Bubby. Adjusting and gently tightening and holding on just enough to burn brightly a little bit longer. Then suddenly, one day, for no particular reason at all... it flickers out.

And I'm left with the love and the light and the love...

KJT 02.27.2020

"Foam"

Grief... always there

Sometimes silent
Creeping
Lurking
Bounding
From nowhere
From somewhere
From everywhere

Slow
Fast
Light
Heavy
Unbearable
Bearable
Until it's not

Near
Smothering
Far
A chasm between
Peace
or calm
Until it's not

Until it closes in
Consuming
Muddling
Distracting
Exhausting
Sucking the very small, weary bit of life
You have left

Bubbling
Bubbling
Up and up and up
Taking the air
The light
The hope
The faith
Forcing you to your knees
Again

Prone
In pain
In agony
In suffering
In surrender
Praying
Praying

Then Faith
Then hope
Then light
Bubbling
Bubbling
Up and up and up
To the very small, weary bit of life you have left

You breathe in
Breathe out
Again
Again
And grief is still here
And you are still here

Searching
Exhausted
Distracted

Muddled
Consumed
With grief

And with life
And light
And love
From nowhere
From somewhere
From everywhere

Love... always there

KJT 03.05.2020

Some days, I don't feel you...

Not my God. Not my Bubby. Only space, then terror. My mind repeatedly wants to return to that moment. To the life-sucking, knee-buckling realization of the unimaginable truth. The instant the world shifted and everything changed. Like the tip of your tongue pressing on a sore tooth... Does it still hurt? More, less, the same? Was it real if I don't feel it right now, feel you right now?

But I know that it is all too real. Just more real at some moments and less at others. The terror. The torture. And I know, too, that I can't keep going back. Can't keep prodding the ache.

So, I move. Each and every morning, I move.

Ever forward so that I don't get stuck. I wake, meditate, pray (most days), cry, open the shades, let the light in, drink my warm lemon water, make my TJ breakfast and just fucking MOVE.

I move for my sanity, for my family, my friends. I move for my Sam. I move to honor him, the mom he believed me to be and to live life two times for him. I move to show anyone who might see, might witness, how God and His infinite love lifts me and moves me. I breathe and remember and smile and laugh and scream and pray and plead and just... move.

And then, I feel you. My God and my Bubby. I feel you in the motion, the trying, the praying, the smiling, the remembering, the laughing and the wailing. In the very act of breathing... I feel you.

And I am reminded... even when I don't see you, you're working. Even when I don't feel you, you're working. So I give you my word, even in those moments...

I'll keep moving!

KJT 03.06.2020

"...At other times it is like being mildly drunk, or concussed. There is a sort of invisible blanket between the world and me."
—C.S. Lewis

When the fog sets in...

I feel as though I am trudging through thigh deep sludge. All the while, my mind is like an old muck-filled pinball machine. Thoughts, ideas, memories, flashbacks, dreams, nightmares, words, screams... all bouncing and ricocheting inside my skull. Heart pounding, exhausted and drained.

What did I say? Who did I see? How did I get here? Both figuratively and sometimes quite literally, how did I get here? What did I eat? Did I eat? I should eat... and wash my hair.

Damn this fog. With its grief and wanting and sadness and guilt and regret and wishing and worry and longing and pleading inhabiting each droplet.

It coats me, covers me, soaks me to my bones. At times. It lifts but is never far from sight, from feeling, confusing and obscuring. It hovers over then closes in, suddenly, with a palpable weight and the muck and mire are too thick. My brain hurts and my body aches.

I am, once again, weighted down and soaking wet with grief.

Smothering, I am surrounded by the fog.

I am told this is normal. That it is to be expected. That it will pass.

So I lean in. I slow down. I pray. I breathe. And search for the light to evaporate the mist and lift the weight.

My dear Jesus is my light. My sweet John is my light. My Sammy's smile and curls and music and art are my light. My Em, Aus, Jess, Aubs, and T are my light. My fluffy pup is my light. My family and friends are my light. My home is my light.

And the fog lifts, if only for a little while, only until next time. But I know for certain, in the back of my mucky, pinball machine mind, that the light is always around me and never far behind.

KJT 03.13.2020

Mandala - a geometric figure representing the universe whose purpose is to help transform the ordinary mind into an enlightened one and to help with healing.

I made this mandala on February 5th.

Two days before Sammy departed on his cosmic journey.

He loved it. In true Sammy form, he was quick to inform me that the "real" mandalas, painstakingly created by monks, are prayed over then destroyed once they are finally finished. That the underlying teaching of the mandala is that change is inevitable and nothing is permanent.

We talked about how cool it would be for me to "deconstruct it" but he thought it too beautiful to destroy. So I gave it to him and he placed it in his cubby in the kitchen.

How was I to know just how impermanent life as I knew it could be? How poignantly, how brutally, how soon the universe would teach me this lesson?

I've seen this piece, proudly displayed in Sam's cubby, for the past 48 days. 48 days. 1,152 hours. 69,120 minutes. 4,147,200 seconds. Each time without my beloved boy. My soulmate.

Life is impermanent. Life is in flux.

It is beautiful and terrible. Full and empty. Colorful and bland. Light and dark. Here then gone.

And so, so worth it.

So today, I embraced the change.

I decided to destroy the mandala that my Bubby so loved. To let it go. To be okay with the temporary. To move ever so slowly forward, knowing that there will be seconds, minutes, hours, days when I will move backwards and be deconstructed... and that's okay.

KJT 03.25.2020

"...the LORD gave, and the LORD has taken away; May the name of the Lord be praised," —Job 1:21

It is the day after my Sam's birthday. Twenty-three minutes after to be exact.

I couldn't/didn't find the energy to write yesterday. I feel as though the universe is waiting. Waiting to see what I might have to say. My people, waiting in all of their love and support and hope and longing that a mama could be okay... on such a day. Or perhaps not...

I've been waiting too. How am I? Is this what okay feels like? Is this numbness? Is this the way it's supposed to feel? Is this honor? Celebration? Pain? Too much? Not enough? What IS this?

It is unnatural. It is surreal. It is okay. It just... is.

It is also the anniversary (weird word) of the day of the passing of my Abuela Fefa and John's Abuelo Feliciano. Big day apparently.

Josephine Rodriguez Haya passed away on April 6, 1993. One year later, on April 6, 1994, my Bubby, Samuel Ellis Davis graced the planet earth. And oddly, on April 6, 2012, Sabino Feliciano Fernandez left these earthly bounds to be with his beloved Nori.

April the 6th... what IS it about that date? I truly cannot say. It seems as though it is a day of great loss and great gifts. It is, quite frankly, a day like any other. A day filled with sorrow and joy. A day filled with remembrances. Sammy never knew Abuela Fefa, but oh, how he was like her. Headstrong, precocious, temperamental, and fiercely loyal to family.

He did, however, know John's Abuelo Feliciano. And oh, how he loved and admired him. Loving, stubborn, honorable, strong, and also fiercely loyal to family.

I suppose there is a teaching there. A reminder. Every day is like April the 6th. Every day is one of joy and sorrow. Gain and loss. Blessing and pain. Some of these, all of these, or a combination of these. Just a day. The gift of another day.

So on THIS April the 6th we remembered our Bubby. Our precocious, beautiful, brilliant, temperamental, stubborn, headstrong, honorable, loving, strong, creative, imaginative and fiercely loyal son, brother, cousin, nephew, grandson and friend. We remembered him by planting a golden rain tree in the front yard of the Compound. We ate fried eggs and rice, papas fritas, and salad, and drank a toast to him for his first birthday in Heaven.

And we gave thanks. Thanks for the peace he now rests in and that he and Abuela Fefa, Abuelo Feliciano, his beloved Abuela Hilda and so many, many more are together and fiercely and forever loving us from afar.

Happy Happy Birthday, my Bubby! You are missed and loved so, so very much... but you know that.

KJT 04.07.2020

"For He will command His angels concerning you to guard you in all your ways." —Psalm 91:11

Cover - to place something over or upon, as for protection.

I had a panic attack last Friday. The third since my Sammy left. The third in my life. It came at me like an encroaching mist. From behind me. Then surrounding me. Then crushing me... quite literally driving me to the floor. The floor of the Walmart self-checkout coral.

Terrific.

Dizzy, heart pounding like a pile driver, limbs numb, sparkles before my eyes, disassociated from my body yet locked in fear. Fear of nothing and everything. Fear of masked faces everywhere. Of bodies anxiously bobbing and weaving away from one another as they pass in the aisles. Berating one another for ignoring the newly applied ENTER and DO NOT ENTER green and red stickers on the floor. Anxiety and confusion permeating the air. My heart, suddenly painfully reminded and aware that Sammy won't be home when we get there. Sammy won't be home ever again.

My mind decided it had simply had quite enough of all of it. So it checked out. Right there in the Walmart self-checkout coral.

Perfect.

Thankfully, my John was with me and pulled down a chair, from a tower of chairs, in the now shuttered Walmart Subway.

So I sat. As John gathered our groceries from the coral, I sat. Prickly, icy, white knuckle hands clutching my knees. Focusing on my 4:4:8 breathing, I sat. Terror growing and swirling around me, within me, I sat. Trying to breathe and calm my hammering heart, I sat. Resisting the cry from every cell in my body to get up and bolt, I sat. To vanish the notion that I might, indeed, be dying in the Walmart.

Fantastic.

I thought about Bubby. How there was NO WAY he was ready for me. About how I could not leave my John, my kids, my family, my friends.

And just then... they covered me.

The angels, the energy, the hope. I envision them in my prayers and meditations. When the despair creeps in at bedtime and I miss my boy so very desperately. Deep in my bones. So deeply that I physically ache for him. My arms remembering so vividly, so clearly what it felt like to hug him. When, in the middle of the night, I am jolted awake by the sound of his voice saying, "Hey, Mom." His sweet voice now only in my dreams. Only in my heart.

They cover me... and we sit.

And ever so slowly my drumbeat heart begins to quiet. My breathing deepens. And we sit.

The mist, the numbness, the sparkles, the dread all begin to dissipate, to lift away. As we sit.

Then there I am. Not dying in the Walmart coral. Alive in the Walmart Subway.

Head clearing, thinking, breathing. Knowing. Knowing that this is all a lot. So much, too much. This shite year 2020.

As we sit.

I asked my John to drop me off at the emergency room. Alone yet not alone, to make certain that I'm not going anywhere any time soon. That I am well.

And I am. Well.

I am loved and healthy and fed and safe and happy and sad and exasperated and hopeful.

And always, always covered.

KJT 04.29.2020

"Sister"

SISTER

not blood of my blood
but heart of my heart
not bone of my bone
but soul of my soul

SISTER

dream believer
boundary stretcher
strength builder
spirit lifter
joy retriever
tear catcher
belly laugher
Friday church attender
wine drinker

SISTER

not blood of my blood
but heart of my heart
not bone of my bone
but soul of my soul

SISTER

respected
beloved
thoughtful
daring
caring
seeking

learning
teaching
loving
lifting

SISTER

child of God
wife
mother
daughter
friend
forgiven
forgiver

SISTER

not blood of my blood
but heart of my heart
not bone of my bone
but soul of my soul

my chosen

SISTER

KJT 07.09.2020

Today I sit to write. Intentionally. With nothing in particular to say yet so much swirling around and clogging my mind. It is always there. A jumbled, insistent, needy, demanding presence. It is too loud. Everything is too loud. And the pressure... so much pressure. Figuratively and now quite literally. In my head, my eyes. Pressure to get this all done. Whatever "this" is. Pressure to heal, to create, to write, but not to paint. No, not to paint.

Painting, the very notion, that way of expressing myself feels daunting and dead. I don't know when or why this has happened. There is nothing there. For now. Hopefully.

I am not happy. I am not unhappy. At times, there is joy and laughter and relaxation, but not deep down. Not in a truthful place.

In the snow, at Sammy's favorite waterfall... that was happiness. As best I can recall. It was quiet, there, in the snow.

I no longer know myself. I am surviving. I am trying. Not thriving. Existing. Floating, sometimes. Confused and lacking curiosity. Stuck. Deconstructing and anticipating the end and then the beginning.

But this end, the imaginary line or date is not an ending. There is no ending. So, is there a beginning? Always feels like sometimes and sometimes feels like never. This fabricated "end" my whirling mind has penned will come and go again and again forever and ever and ever. Will it be different? It will be different, to be sure. Less than? Better? Easier? No. Or yes. Or maybe. I do not know.

I do know that I am trying. I am working. I am tired. A lot. I need more quiet but don't know how to get it, where to find it. There is so much to say. To spill out and let go of.

Yet, I have little to give. As I hurtle and drift at once towards the end that is not the end. This is the noise and pressure within.

I will take the time. I will do the work. I will still the noise and be as honest as I can be.
Until I find the joy, deep down in a truthful place.

KJT 01.21.2021

Anniversaries, old pictures, bombs.

As we get closer to the one-year anniversary (anniversary... such a conflicting word for me. It doesn't mean celebration but has most certainly become associated with them.) of my Bubby's passing. I don't say dying. I don't like passing either. I need to find a different word. A word that suits the situation better.

But old pictures. They, too, send different messages these days. Mostly sad. Mostly loss. Baby pictures of the happiest, smiley boy... What happened? Where did he get lost? What did I do, or not do, to make everything not alright? Can't go back. Can't go over it and over it over and over. All I see are so many hopes and dreams I held when I took those pictures of my smiling, happy boy. And suddenly, I am sad because these pictures break my heart. How can such sweet smiles become little, brightly colored instruments of torture? Physical pain deep down in the center of my chest. Tightening. Pounding. Don't look! Don't see! Look away! Skim over. Turn the "I love you, Grandpa" mugs around in the cupboard. But don't throw them away. Don't hide them away. That would be heartbreaking. Mean. Unfair. Unnecessary. Just don't look. Don't see.

Old photos popping up and appearing, like magic, on my phone to show me what I was doing "on this day last year." Anniversary pics of the everyday. Last year. The "what would I have done, could I have done?" if I'd known that I'd only have my boy, that precious face, that sweet smile for just one more month, three more weeks, 15 more days. Time. An unknown countdown. That's what old pictures are to me now, for now. Little, colorful, smiling, hopeful, joy-filled time bombs whispering "What happened, when, why?" Old pictures...

KJT 01.21.2021

"The eye is the lamp of the body. If your eyes are healthy, your whole body will be full of light." —Matthew 6:22

Perception affects everything.

My perception is off. Or stuck. Or negative. How does one perceive the loss of a beautiful soul, your precious child, in a positive light? You can't. You don't. I've tried. The grateful spots, the "what if's," the "it could have been worse"... No. It couldn't have been. I'm too small right now, maybe I always was, to believe in the "big picture." I tell myself, and everyone forced to listen to me, that I am too small in this world, this universe, this time, this grief to even care about a " bigger picture." Small? Petty? Yes! Petty. I am. It is, "of little importance, trivial, lesser of scale, minor" to me. My eyes are not healthy now. Not healthy most days.

And the better days, are those days real? Are they "healthy eye" days? Those days where I can see the "big picture," or at least acknowledge, hope, pray, believe that there is such a thing. That great, beautiful, brilliantly clear and shining "big picture." Where all of the pain and doubt and suffering and loss all magically make sense and I can breathe again. A real breath. Deep and clear and free and natural. An unencumbered breath. An undefended breath. A breath of light. I don't know. Sometimes they are. Maybe.

But when the gut-punch comes from my blindside, sending anguish surging through every cell, my eyes go dim. His smile, his joy, his laugh, his voice, his scent, the feel of his hug, the way he crossed his big toe, his birthmark, and so many hopes and dreams... all gone. Forever. For always.

My eyes are unhealthy. I am searching for the light.

KJT 01.28.2021

"More"

Anxious
A little
Buzzing
Deep down
Inside

Quiet
But there
Always
At once Demanding
Distractable

Flushing
Sadness up
Reminding
Chastising
Mustn't forget

While laughing
And living

For what
For whom
Not me
Not you

For you
Missing
And longing
And remembering
And smiling

More
And more
For me

For you

Anxious
But less
And hoping
For more

More freedom
More joy
More light
More air
More life
More good

More memories
Of you

KJT 02.05.2021

Today is a better day. As days go. As the day I anticipated dread, at once, creeps closer. I am a runaway. An avoider. In hiding. Walking miles per day to "exercise." Both, maybe. The sunlight and water and birds and wind serve with purposes as I move through them mile after mile. Going away but really nowhere at all. Listening to my audiobooks for escape. Vanishing into other people's stories, whether real or make believe, all the while seeking out and hoping for the answer, the explanation, the hidden meaning of all of this. My all too real life. I don't have it. God's not talking. At least not directly. To me. Perhaps there are glimmers in the stories and words and memories and imaginations and hopes and dreams and miracles and losses of others. Some whispers between the lines or a shout that leaps from the page and through my earbuds that will help me adjust. Move forward. Look ahead. Be in the moment. Find hope. Experience gratitude. Remember the good stuff. That I am good. A good mom. His good mom. An "ah-haaa!" nugget to help make each day a tiny bit brighter. Like today. This day. Slowly, quickly approaching THE day. But today. Today is a better day.

KJT 02.05.2021

"The Nothing"

Sometimes...
I have no words
Quite literally

Nothing
Silence
Blankness

They won't come
Don't come
Can't come

They jumble
Stumble
Skip over

Thoughts one to the other
Frustrated
Concerned
Angry

It's too loud
In the nothing

There's too much
In the nothing

I can't
Conjure the words
Can't bring them forth

Coherently
Calmly
Quietly

Shouting

Guilty
Ashamed

Be still
It's okay
Be kind

To myself
For myself

Listen
For the words
Or the absence of them

Be still, kind, patient
It's okay
Keep working

In the nothing.

KJT 02.25.2021

"Going"

I am going
leaving
heading out
for a few days

To go inside
the deep down
within

To find you
To find me
To find us

I am excited
nervous
looking forward
to going back
to now
to then
to tomorrow

To what is
what was
what could be
should be
but isn't
won't be
can't be
is

So I am going
but am not gone
to seek
to find
to learn

to grow

And you
you are here

KJT 02.28.2021

"Bayou Mourn"

Greys
Grasses
Marshes
Mud
Mint tea
Steaming
Cool air
Musty
Salty
Life
Chirping
Buzzing
Squawking
Flapping
Misty rain
Drip
Drip
Dripping
Breeze
Blowing
Tickling
Lifting
Birds
Large
Small
Osprey
Eagle
Heron
Crow
Playing
Soaring
Hunting
Fishing
Living

In the greys
In the grasses
In the marshes
In the mud
Living
Thriving
Being
Here
Now
On this
Bayou mourn

KJT   03.02.2021

"Perdition"

I found you, on that morning
Curled up against the wall
The fact that you had left me
Did not make sense at all

We'd just been loving, laughing
Now your balled up on the floor
I never thought my world would change
When I stepped through your door

There is a sound, what is it
A cry, a scream, a shout
It comes from deep inside my soul
I cannot make it out

It is my heart, my wailing soul
That won't be silenced now
For joy and hope and peace and rest
My pain will not allow

KJT 03.03.2021

43

"Noise"

There's constant noise
Inside my head
And in my soul
I feel this dread

Cacophony
That will not cease
My mind, my heart
They yearn for peace

I walk, I drive,
I meditate
Persistent clamor
Seems my fate

Yet, oh, those sounds
I yearn to hear
Like distant thunder
Drawing near

Or crashing waves
And rustling leaves
Embracing me
Then I can breathe

Slow and deep
And out and in
So I can hear
The me within

KJT 03.09.2021

"You"

Sadness
Comes
Sometimes
Anew
As if it were
The first day
Hour
Minute
Second
Without you

Here
Really here
In the flesh
Where
I can hold
Feel
See
Hear
Breathe
You

Opaque
This grief
At once
Blinding
Dark
Carried
But not
Released
Resounding
Without you

Emerging

From nowhere
Everywhere
Sometimes
Softer
Gentle
Reminder
Of loss
Love
You

Forever
And always
Now
And again
While living
Growing
Learning
Moving
Forward
Without you

Changing
Always
Painfully
Completely
Though healing
Slowly
Awkwardly
Purposefully
Because of
You

KJT 03.16.2021

"TODAY"

This
Offering
Divinely
Afforded
You

This
Only
Day
Allowed
Yet

The
One
Delight
Already
Yours

Thankfully
Originally
Designed
As
Yours

The
Offered
Day
After
Yesterday

Thwarted
Ornery
Downtrodden
Always

Yielding

Temporal
Often
Dwelling
Always
Yearning

KJT 03.20.2021

"The Missing"

It comes, the missing
Not in waves
But as a white-hot point of light
Yet unable to pierce the darkness

Expanding and swelling
Deep within my heart and soul
Consuming every cell
Of my marrow, of my being

It is gnawing and nagging, the missing
Fervent and impenetrable
As a dank woolen blanket
Shrouding me from head to foot

In a sorrow that can't be shaken
A torment that won't be loosed
An emptiness with mass
A burden forever borne

The world is dark, in the missing
Colorless and tragic
I trudge slowly through it
With great effort just to breathe

Just to be
To see through the gloom
Of weeping eyes
Engorged with grief

A well-spring of tears, is the missing
Seeping endlessly down pallid cheeks
Pooling near my heart
Where they feel at home

Pouring and pouring
Striving to extinguish
Both the ache and the heat
Now blazing within and throughout

Until their source runs dry, from the missing
And I detect small rays of light and flecks of color
And I breathe an air less thick
Less burdened by my grief-drenched cloak

Looking clear-eyed, for now
At my life going forward
On a world spinning on
A world where my beloved boy, is missing

KJT 03.30.2021

I suffer a constant companion. A cohort and an accomplice in my life made over. Attending me on the good days and enveloping me on the bad. Orchestrating both the joyous and the unbearable. Always hovering just above the light. At times, with density decreasing, it doesn't encroach into every thought and allows a bit more color to break through. Slowly though, as if feeding of any notion of bliss, any fancy of peace, it becomes heavy-laden. Graying and clamoring to be seen. "What is that?" I ponder, as the faint shadows around a contented moment begin to lengthen, the light sluggishly dipping behind unseen trees. My heart, crumbling again beneath the weight of the thickening mist. My soul, at once, recognizes the source. My grief, its wellspring. "So that is what it is"... my little black cloud. It represents the ever-present conflict of my new existence that fluctuates between smiles and tears. A state of being that is utterly beyond my control. So, I sit in the ensuing downpour, observing as it bleeds itself dry. Resting, even, in the deluge as it slowly cleanses away fragments of my pain bit by bit, drop by drop. And eventually, some light breaks through. Tiny prisms of hope. Hope that my little black cloud will grow smaller as the minutes, hours, days tick by. Becoming but a whisp of its present self. I succumb to the truth that it will always be with me. That it is a part of me now. Knowing too, that it will not consume me but instead serve to remind me that I walked through the suffering and the shadows and came out into the light.

KJT 05.11.2021

Missing you is a phantom pain. My body aches for the feel of your long, nimble arms wrapped around my shoulders in a big bear hug. I miss the smell of your skin and the feel of your whiskers as I smooched your beautiful face. The scent of your hair, in a tiny treasure box on my bedside table, is absent of your warmth. I miss you in my bones that ache with the thought of you being gone. Being here without you has changed my physical being. There is a piece of my heart ripped away. There are cells of my cells forever gone. As I struggle to heal, I can feel the scar tissue repairing and making me stronger, but it doesn't feel a part of me yet. I don't recognize its fibrous texture growing in flesh and spirit. It remains a foreign body within me, and I am a stranger to myself. A phantom of whom I once was.

KJT 04.12.2022

"Untethering"

In the beginning
Before I could see you
Growing
Thriving
And oh, so small
I knew you were there

Part of me
One with me

Tethered together

Before I could feel you
Kicking
Rolling
Curled beneath my heart
I knew you were there

For such a short time
Until it was ripe for you
To come
Into this world
Into my arms
No longer beneath
But forever in
My heart

Tethered together

When you could toddle
Then walk
Then run
You moved so quickly
Away from me

But never far
Before looking back
To me
For me
My hand
You knew I was there

Tethered together

As you grew
With dreams
With ideas
With plans
Of your own
We loved and we fought
And moved
Away
Towards
The new
The growing
The thriving
Life you chose
You knew I was there

Still tethered together

Then
You were gone
Away
For always
And forever

How I long to touch you
To hear your heart
That is my heart
No longer beneath
But forever in

To hear your voice
To smell your skin
To see your eyes
Brown
Clear
Knowing
Are you still there

With love
In grief
I keep you

Tethered together

But now
For you
For me
I fear
And regret
That our tethering
Keeps you bound
To me
To my sorrow
My anguish
And prevents
Your new life
New world
New adventures
From being realized

So I untether
For you, my boy
Will continue
Expanding
Transfiguring
Becoming

In this beginning
Though I can no longer see you
Growing
Thriving
And oh, so grand
I hope you are here

Still part of me
Still one with me

Untethered together

KJT 04.23.2021

"With Me"

I awaken
slowly
as the milky blue light
begins to break
it cracks me open
suddenly, forcefully
the remembering
that you are not here

I shudder
tremulously
as the opaque dread
shrouds and constricts me
leaden and alive
the grieving
that you are gone

I walk
purposefully
as the damp morning
drains my essence
vapidly, piece by piece
the anguish
of missing you

I cry out
silently
as tears overflow their brim
cool and briny
the sorrow of longing for you

I move forward
arduously
as the wind picks up

playful and enticing
the hope
that you are near

I startle
skittishly
as a cloud grey dolphin
breaches
the surface
beckoning me, cajoling
to recognize
that you are with me

I laugh
tearfully, joyfully
as grace envelopes me
tender and steadfast
with encouragement
of your enduring lifeforce

I run
chasing awkwardly
as your spirit embodied
glides and whirls and splashes
the showing of your impish spirit

I slow
winded and energized
as a glistening tail slaps farewell
swishing and sharing
the reassurance
that we will meet again

KJT 05.04.2021

"Loom"

frayed and undone
like a cast-off clump of yarn
this life distorted
the air
heavy
thick
unrecognizable
the future
a great expanse
seen through the fog
gauzy and unknown
yet interlaced
with hope and possibility
all weaving together
the fabric of a life anew
prismatic and complex
in and out
and up and down
and back and forth
until
a new material is rendered
mended and reborn

KJT 05.07.2021

"Fragment"

The ceiling of the world cracked
and came crashing down
on that day
upon me

Little jagged pieces of mirrored glass
laying at my feet
on my knees
face down

Everywhere I looked
I could only see pieces of me
crushed and strewn about
like tiny shards of grief

At first, I walked gingerly
so as not to crush any more
tiny shattered bits
of me

But then, one day, they caught the light
in just the right way
so that I could see the beauty
in the debris

So I gathered up each piece
every one a little bit of me
of the shiny, beautiful life
that once was

And began to put the broken pieces
back together again
one shard at a time
carefully, gently

Until the ceiling was rebuilt
broken but shining and reflecting the light
in a million different directions
brilliant and new

KJT 06.10.2021

"The Spot"

Breeze
blowing
waves
lapping
sunlight
shimmering
on the surf
through the fronds

Friends
gathered
together
laughing
dancing
in the sand
on the shore

Sunday morning
shining
bright
breakfast
cooking
on the grill
by the sea

Together
grateful
thankful
for years past
for years
to come

KJT 07.19.2021

"Forward"

forward facing
onward moving
striving daily
to fly

going to
not leaving from
seeking now
to thrive

breath by breath
and step by step
with love
along the way

embrace each moment
explore the wonder
and live
just for today

KJT 09.19.2021

"Porch Thoughts"

not yet whole
but a part
like the rising sun
not yet whole
but bright
and full of potential
not yet whole
but slowly spreading warmth and light
across an ever-expanding space
not yet whole
but soon to be
over and over and over
not yet whole
but still me

KJT 11.27.2021

"Thanksgiving 2021"

early morning departure as the autumn sun rises
cars and hearts packed to the brim
with groceries, warm clothes and anticipation
hours of classic tunes play
as daylight turns from full to dappled to barely there
a fuchsia stripe beneath a bruised blue sky

white, warm farmhouse atop a rolling hill
home for a little while
full of family, friends, and food
the clear, crisp days lull by
and morph into star filled night
in kitchen and on porch
bundled together and warmed by fire and gratitude

bright kitchen, warm ovens, mimosas all around
turkey day aprons and pj's adorn
awaiting Santa's first glimpse
turkey, butter, flour, sugar,
beans, squash, onions and garlic
mix with laughter and Christmas music

the feast, the love, the wine
fill our bellies and souls
fireside naps, marshmallows toasting and endless
boardgames
as time breathes slowly by for one more day

early morning departure as the autumn sun rises
cars and hearts packed to the brim
with leftovers, dirty laundry
and a lifetime of memories

KJT 11.30.2021

Another year gone, without you. Another year crawling by. Another year that feels like forever. Another year that you didn't come back. Another year that you are truly gone. Not away on some grand adventure only to return one day, one year, ever. I, my mind, cannot comprehend, cannot bend itself around the blank space that your precious presence has left behind. Another year my weary soul recoils from the heavy, unyielding, tangible heat of your absence. Another year I missed everything about you. The scent of your hair and skin as I smooched your beautiful face. The sound of your voice. The way you crossed your big toe over the others, as you watched your favorite shows, and crumpled the napkin from your meal into the tiniest ball in your long-fingered hand. Another year to be afraid that you are not only gone, but fading away. Another year that I love you more and more and more and forever and ever and ever. Another year rolling into the next and more of the same.

KJT 12.31.21

Broken – sEPARATED iNTO pARTS
- dAMAGED oR aLTERED
- hAVING uNDERGONE oR sUBJECTED tO fRACTURE
- nOT wORKING pROPERLY
- bEING iRREGULAR, iNTERRUPTED, fULL oF oBSTACLES
- vIOLATED bY tRANSGRESSION
- dISRUPTED bY cHANGE
- mADE wEAK oR iNFIRM
- sUBDUED, cOMPLETELY cRUSHED, sORROWFUL
- cUT oFF, dISCONNECTED
- nOT cOMPLETE oR fULL
- dISUNITED bY sEPARATION

I am broken. I am "all of the above". These words fit me like a well-worn glove as I continue to navigate the world in deepest grief. Twenty-three months later, I move through time and space, at once, slowly and quickly. The workings of my mind not recognizing and recording the passage of time in any frame of reality or normalcy as it frantically, erratically pulls and pushes me through each day, each moment, each second. I move too quickly, talk too fast, my mind and body buzzing and racing at an unhealthy frequency. I can feel heartbreak changing me, altering my cells, my marrow. I am disjointed and inflamed in form and spirit, aching and crying out for relief as I drown in the tears of my sorrow. I am weary to the bone... but I am also resolute. The exhaustion and pain demand to be dealt with, confronting me at every turn. Promises I made to Sammy force their way through the darkness that consumes me. My words play back to me: "I will live two times for you," "I will find joy again," "I will make this world a kinder place." So, there are decisions to make that must be made each day, each moment. I will strive to fulfill these promises, for Sammy, for me, and for my tribe. I will put in the work, nourish my body and feed my soul. I have reached out for help and will accept it with a grateful heart. And I will try, oh how I'll try, to see and welcome the light that is patiently waiting to shine through the cracks of my brokenness.

KJT 01.06.2022

"Shroud"

grief dons many cloaks
at once
they are weighty and dank
dulled and feathery
always in flux

at times
these shrouds are neatly tucked away
hanging upon stakes through a broken heart
accumulating into unruly heaps

alternating
between emptiness and ache
anger and envy
terror and tears

anguish
wraps itself tightly in layers
suffocating
spirit and will
flesh and bone
hopes and dreams

sapping
energy and courage
creativity and mischief
joy and light

struggling
to be seen
to be known
to be loosed

this devastation strangles like a creeping vine

imperceptibly
encroaching upon every thought
expanding through body and mind
winding about the edges of sanity

propagating
guilt
and shame
and self-doubt

altering
memory
and vision
and truth

until
forever evolving
grief begins to shed its gruesome shrouds
through great effort and will
in graceful surrender
slowly
methodically
piece by dreadful piece

intentionally changing
by faith
with hope
in love

reluctantly resolving
to, once again, be hung
tentatively
upon the pegs
of a now resilient
healing
heart
KJT 01.18.2022

"I Love…"

I love the space of nothingness
between wake and sleep
The feeling of deep relief
and peace that exists in that darkness

I love icy-cold, clear mornings
so crisp and bright
that you can almost see
the endless possibilities flitting about
in the air

I love my dog curled up at my feet
on watch
for everything and nothing
full of loyalty and love

I love winter's bare branches
against a cobalt blue sky
transforming forest lattice
into cathedral windows

I love the sting and tickle in my nose
of crisp, dry, morning air
as I breathe in
a new day

I love how my pup's ears twitch
ever so slightly
at every pip, chirp, caw
that floats across
the morning breeze

I love being dressed in layers
of flannel and fur

still feeling the frigid air
between and surrounding
being just shy of warm

I love the feel of butterflies
in joyful anticipation
of the day ahead
of adventures to come

I love the rose that blooms
on my cheeks from the cold
only to blossom
by the warmth of the fire

I love slowly rocking
to the sound
of nothing

I love listening to the popping of ice
and berries pelting
the dry forest floor
Or the cracking of acorns
in chubby chipmunk cheeks
And not really knowing
or caring
which it truly is

I love...
all these things
and more
And so grateful
that I can

KJT 01.21.2022

"Me"

who am I
now
without you

not real
me
this existence

without you
now
I am

it is
forever
without you

me in you
you in me
me

KJT 03.30.2022

"Night"

warm bed
contentedly tired
eyelids flutter
fading into sleep
"I miss you, my boy"
deep recessesd
stir to life
stretch and awaken
releasing disbelief
impossibilities
realities
endless
painful truths
"I see you, grief"
"Come in and sit for a while"
begging
pleading
praying
to see you, Bubby
talk to you
in a dream
in this nightmare
visions spiral and morph
until nothing
and all of it
combine
into a silent scream
hair clutching
and body curled
then darkness comes
and eyelids flutter
exhausted
into a warm, tearstained bed
KJT 05.05.2022

"Summer Fun"

Sitting on the porch
of a cabin
on a river
quiet
birds calling
crickets chirping
puppy at my feet
watching for squirrels
panting

Shoulders
sun kissed
from a morning
on the current
through ancient woods
drifting
floating
breathing

Afternoon walk
majestic oaks
shading
towering
while cypress knees
hold court
over spongy ground

Friends gather
a different porch
telling stories
belly laughing
sharing secrets
sipping wine
and icy beer

Relaxing
making fire
burgers grilling
marshmallows toasting
sitting amidst the golden glow

Staring
into the embers
sweating
in the heat
of the flames
and muggy night

A perfect end
to the beginning
of summer fun

KJT 06.04.2022

There are words inside of me, jumbled and needing to get out yet not truly wanting to. I exist behind an invisible wall that stands inside my mind. It is not new, just back again, and more subtle than its previous incarnations. It leaves me unsure and unable to see the "me" on the other side. My grief is changing. Not as omnipresent and oppressive, but arriving in rolling, crestless waves that slowly lap back to where they started. A lazy river of sadness that runs through a verdant forest blooming with new hopes and dreams and the sense that I am going to be more than okay. Forever changed and wonderful.

KJT 06.17.2022

"Inside My Head"

I scream inside my head sometimes
a howl without sound
I watch myself
from outside myself
writhing
on my knees
fists pound upon the ground

I scream inside my head sometimes
at a god who is not there
knowing they do not understand
this suffering mess
broken
bloodied
and stripped bare

I scream inside my head sometimes
sheer blackness in my view
breathing slower
all cried out
exhausted
spent
in hope of something new

KJT 09.12.2022

"Still"

Like the water of the bay
motionless and flat
I am still

Like silver gray clouds
that mottle sky and surface
I hover between shadow and light

As damp morning air
blankets skin and bone
I listen to silence for the sound of your voice

As calm and tranquility
sparkle before searching eyes
I wrestle with absence

Like dawn turns to day
continuously, faithfully, for always
I miss you

Still

KJT 02.06.2023

"The Fact of It"

Tell me, dear one, who do you love

Why, I love him

I love his soul
The warmth of it
The depth of it
The pure and simple fact of it

I love his nature
The calmness of it
The kindness of it
The strong and faithful fact of it

I love his heart
The tenderness of it
The capacity of it
The constant and calming fact of it

I love his strength
The gentleness of it
The steadiness of it
The quiet and patient fact of it

I love his love
The joy of it
The passion of it
The deep and abiding fact of it

I love HIM entirely
The light in him
The darkness in him
The forever and always fact of him

That, dear one, is who I love

KJT 02.14.2023

"Waiting"

Mockingbird
sings his song
the melodies of others
beautifully
cheerfully

Tiny thief
chirps above
the city streets
bustle
and din

Spirited caroler
purposefully roosts
on branch or wire
gleeful
and determined

Limerent crooner
calls out
mournfully
for her
from dawn to dawn

Ambitious lover
tirelessly serenades
his consort
departed
or not yet found

Mockingbird
sings his song
the melodies of others
longingly

he waits

KJT 02.22.2023

"Awakening"

Dawn
upon me
through my window
of my mind

Becoming
light
outside
and within

Flushing
space and time
with golden
knowing

Changing
slowly
purposefully
into a new day

KJT 02.25.2023

"If Wishes Fell Like Rain"

If wishes fell like rain
then certainly I am a storm
Sodden droplets filled with pain
swirl 'round me like a swarm

If wishes fell like rain
mine would fill a vast blue sea
Each and every wish would be
to bring you back to me

If wishes fell like rain
in time the clouds would part
The sun would one day shine again
with you forever in my heart

KJT 02.27.2023

"Uncle"

"We lost your Uncle Larry"
was all my father said
Disbelief and anger
roiled 'round my weary head

The message from my uncle
just 10 short days ago
feels like a premonition
It was his time now to go

I felt it then, I knew it
though I pushed it from my mind
Sometimes the soul is seeing
while the body remains blind

I cannot finish writing
there's just too much to say
My heart filled up with emptiness
as another has gone away

KJT 02.28.2023

"The Still"

The wind is blowing
off the bay
The choppy waves
crash against the shore
the sea wall
I cannot smell the salt today
the scent that feels like home

The sun is hot on my skin
it stings but shouldn't
Not in this October light
low and sideways

Birds swoop and chirp overhead
but I prefer the quiet ones
Like soldiers in a row
they sit upon the dock
perched low into the wind
Silent, observing
hunkered down in the beauty of the day

KJT 02.28.2023

"Sit"

I sit
with Sadness
on my porch
in the billowing breeze.

Awful companion
"Greetings and salutations.
Come in
and stay awhile."

"I will not fight
push
or wish
you away."

Begrudgingly welcome,
my new escort,
as a reminder
of infinite love.

So I sit
with Sadness
on my porch
until the billowing breeze whisks you away.

KJT 03.13.2023

"Confession"

I must acknowledge something
of the changing that's inside
I do not recognize me
as I'm tossed about this tide

Grief flows and churns and swirls about
and changes day by day
like swooping, squawking sea birds
as they soar above the bay

Most know of my great sorrow
they've been with me all along
they love, support and lift me
and help me to be strong

But what I must confess now
is that I do not know myself
it's as though the me that was me
has been tossed upon a shelf

Ripped away from normal
and the world that I had known
to be beat against the rocks of pain
and left here all alone

I do not share this stranger
she's protected safe within
resting, watching, growing
so that I can be again

Who or what I do not know
I'm working every day
to find myself and figure out
just what she has to say

So this is my confession
my struggle and my strife
to find a way to joy and peace
in this brand-new life

KJT 03.14.2023

"State of Being"

We dream with hearts
Wide open
We live with minds
Clamped tight
Our breath the only savior
to bring darkness into light.

KJT 03.22.2023

"We Are"

We are
Not apart
But a part

We are
Separated
But not separate

We are
Complete
But not finished

KJT 03.25.2023

"Healing"

Slowing down and filling up
Up where serenity begins
Begins to heal heart and soul
Mind worn and ill at ease
Ease the frantic need to do
Do that which brings you joy
Joy in the undoing
Undoing what's been done
Done with racing life and heart
Heart and soul are slowing
Slowing down and filling up

KJT 03.27.2023

"I Know"

Beloved, I know

I know your scream
the wail within your chest
that beats against your ribs
and steals your very breath away

May the love of those around you cradle your
tender, ravaged heart.

Beloved, I know

I know your anguish
the wide, horror filled eyes
blind with grief
searching for the beauty of your baby's face

May the memories, too painful to see right now, one
day surround you and lift you to a place of joy.

Beloved, I know

I know your disbelief
the bolt of lightning
that rips through body and mind
with the continuous realization that they have gone on

May the passage of time and the mystery of hope carry
you to merciful acceptance.

Beloved, I know

I know your terror
the fear of sleep's respite
that gives way to agony
upon the opening of weary eyes

May you find rest and support in the arms of those who
love and keep you and yours.

Beloved, I know

I know your confusion
of a tomorrow without your child
that simply cannot be
but heartbreakingly is

May your murkiness of spirit give way
to minutes, then hours, then days of clarity and light.

Beloved, I know

I know your rage
the roiling, messy hatred
that fills your heart and mind
and drags you to the brink of sanity

May your heart find comfort and relief in the act of release.

Beloved, I know

I know the stranger
deep in your cells and marrow
who has seized your very soul
forever changing who you are

May you come to know and love and accept the transfigured
being you are becoming.

Beloved, I know

I know your prayers
the screaming, anguished, disbelieving,
terror-filled, confused and rageful lamentations
that feel hollow and unheard

May the whole of your experience be seen, validated and
honored and may love encompass and heal all that you are.

Beloved, I know

KJT 03.28.2023

"Bravery"

To be brave
Is to love yourself
In spite of

KJT 03.31.2023

"Flow"

Ancient
Packed
Otherworldly blue
Pressure
Building
Creaking
Groaning
Moving
Imperceivably
But not
For us
Breaking
Crashing
Thunder
Echoing
Renewal
Again
For eons
For you
For me
Forever
She flows

KJT 05.05.2024

"Verdure"

Vibrant greens
In dappled sunlight
From the shade
Around your bench

Your favorite colors
Alive and aglow
In the steamy morn
Beneath grandfather boughs

Chartreuse and lime
Basil and moss
Embrace and soothe
A grief drenched spirit

Shimmering light
Flickers through leaves
And illuminates hope
And red-headed messengers

A verdant balm for the ache
Quiets the scream
And reminds the heart
That you're still here

KJT 06.27.2024

"Babe"

A masterpiece
Of sinew and bone
Pushed forth into life
With shuttering breath

From outstretched toes
On wrinkled feet
To silken whorls
On velvet crown

New mother sways
As newly opened ocean eyes
Take in the mystery
Of her glow

KJT 07.23.2024

"The Guide"

A vision bright
Stands tall and slight
With hair of gold
Or is it white?

Their back to me
A he, a she
In gleaming light
I cannot see

Questions float in balmy air
Of feelings not so often shared
With breathless hope
I dream, I dare

Is this an angel
Sent to me?
Ancestral guide
To set me free?

Free from guilt
From loss and pain
Transcendent love
Gives life again

They bend before
A babbling brook
And dip their hand
I kneel to look

Water whorls
Around and through
Fluorescent fingers
I know not who

"Be like the brook"
They say to me
"Let go, let go"
"You shall be free"

A loving guide
Through time and space
Appeared to me
And gave me grace

KJT 10.28.2024

"Flutter"

Just a little tumble
Head over heart
A flash of light
"There"
Or here
No fear
Nor sorrow
Confusion?
No...
Curiosity
And unknowing
The unknowable
Now knowable

Magic and wonder
Timelessness
Weightlessness
The colors of music
The sounds of light
The everything
The everywhere
The everyone
The joy
The peace
The love
In the flutter

KJT 10.31.2024

"The Magnet Screen"

I look for you
Everywhere
In everything

On the wind
In the rustling leaves
And dappled light

In dolphin flips
Pink bellies bared
And osprey calls
And shimmies

In the beat
Of the woodpeckers' work
And the sparkle
Of a brown squirrel's eye

In cloud formations
As they move across the sky
And feathers abandoned
On the ground

This side of the magnet screen
Where it seems like magic
Or a tiny cosmic miracle

Your enduring energy
Inhabiting everything
The little, wonderous things
For a moment in time

Unaware
The screen betwixt

Space and time
Snaps shut

Between you
And I
Your part of the everything
And mine
For a moment
I don't feel
The gaping hole that fills
Where you once lived

Can you see me
Through the film
Do you know
When I ache the most

I wish to leap
With desperation
And hope
Through the fissures that you make

Yet I can't
Not yet
So please
Keep finding me

Until I can find you
On your side
Of the magnet screen

KJT 11.16.2024

"November Pain"

I still believe
Don't I?
That love wins
Triumphs
Over hate
And negativity
And entitlement

But not for now
Not today

So go deep
Where the darkness lies
The world's darkness
My darkness
Cells on fire
In fear
Skin bristling
With anxiety

In the desolation
Of loves absence
So valiantly
Fought off
Walked with
And through
Know your heart
Remember your heart
The light you stoke
With jagged breath
Again and again

Never let hate's icy smirk
Extinguish

Your heart's radiant warmth
Because if not now
But later
And always
LOVE>HATE

KJT 11.04.2024

"Obsidian"

Still
Deep breathing
As I enter the home of my being
Gently taking in
All that resides there
Witnessing
That which comes forth

Fear

My nemesis
And old friend
Given form and shape
As I tenderly place it before me
Separate
From me

Oh, sharp black stone
So lovely in your darkness
Reflecting and distorting my image
In your sheen
Threat and suffering
Dance
About your sharp edges
They cut me with thoughts
That come alive at night

I resist and push against
Your weight and dominion
Becoming a friction
Of anxiety and panic
That envelopes and swirls about
The manifestation of my dread
Slowly becoming hotter

Before my glistening eyes

A flame
In the absence of my breath
A piece of candescent carbon
Flourishing in my opposition

I breathe
I release
I breathe
I release
I observe
As the edges begin to soften
As I allow my breath
To flow past it
And encircle it
As tears begin to fall
Relief made manifest
In the water of life

They cool the flame
That defiance has stoked
A chemical reaction
Of fear with acceptance
And breath with release
Births something anew

A rainbow stone lies
Before me
Filled with color and light
Built of fire and water
That I return to my home
Within

An iridescent seed
Of my completeness
Ever growing and changing

Glowing and illuminating
This beautiful life
As I carry on

KJT 01.14.2025

"For Good"

We traveled together
My sisters
My brothers
My love
To a beautiful place
Nearly erased
By a deluge
From above

We journeyed together
With joy
With hope
With pain
At a sacred time
With Sammy in mind
A sweet soul
That remains

We trekked together
To help
To Give
To heal
With funds we'd raised
And thanks and praise
For a love
That is so real

We pilgrimaged together
My sisters
My brothers
My love
To a beautiful place
Rising in grace
To spread

Our Sammy's love

KJT 02.11.2025

"Phosphene"

Is that you?
In the space behind
closed lids
In the white speck
of light
A portal that holds
unknown worlds
rooted in whorls of deep blue
moving about the speckled blackness
that gathers just before sleep

Is this the space?
Where you cross the vale
and wander into dreams
vaguely recalled
and illusive visitations longed for
in nightly prayer

Are you there?
Within the luminescent particle
that fades with focus
Only able to be viewed
with diverted eye
and unchanneled vision
Fading in the striving
for clarity
of where you are

Is that you?
Is this the space?
Are you there?

KJT 03.13.2025

ABOUT THE AUTHOR

Kelly Jo Terry is an artist, writer and seeker who loves to read, travel and learn all she can about the world and its endless mysteries. After years as an early childhood educator and raising her own children, she decided to focus on her art and began painting portraits and landscapes for what would become a long list of clients.

In February of 2020, however, that all changed after the devastating loss of her beloved 25-year-old son. Struggling to make sense of her grief and the new life she found herself thrust into, Kelly Jo began to journal. With all the color drained from her world and her creative spirit gone with her boy, writing of her suffering became her anchor and pen replaced paint brush. Words became guides that would help her navigate life with grief and help her find her creative self once more. She eventually co-authored and illustrated the children's book "Fly Anyway" and has filled more than three journals with poems and prose.

Kelly Jo believes that writing down her most sacred thoughts and feelings saved her life and hopes that her words might be a comfort to others in times of grief.

www.ingramcontent.com/pod-product-compliance
Lightning Source LLC
Chambersburg PA
CBHW071222090426
42736CB00014B/2941